Beaut
and the
BEAST

Retold by Michael Morpurgo
Illustrated by Loretta Schauer

Collins

2

For Marco and his wife and three daughters, life was good.
He was a respected merchant of fine silks, tapestries and spices
from the East. They lived in a grand house in the city and were
healthy, wealthy and happy.

But then, one spring, Marco's wife died suddenly. Marco did his
best to keep his daughters happy. He gave them everything they
asked for; presents every time he came home. The two older
sisters soon became very spoilt.

Only the youngest, Belle, remained loving and kind-hearted.
She always hated it when her father went away to work.
Whenever he wasn't there, her sisters were horrible to her.

So Belle was overjoyed to look out of her window one morning
and see him arriving home sooner than she'd expected.

"Presents!" cried her sisters, and they all ran downstairs
to greet him. But there were no presents.

Marco slumped down in his chair and told them the dreadful news. "All's lost," he said. "The ship carrying all my silks, tapestries and spices has been taken by pirates. We've no money. I shall have to sell everything we own to pay my debts. There'll be no more servants or presents. Those days are over."

"How can we live without servants?" the two older sisters cried.

"From now on," said their father, "we'll have to do everything for ourselves. We'll have to live in a cottage in the mountains, and keep sheep and cows and grow all our own food."

"Mountains, sheep, cows, how wonderful!" Belle cried. But her two sisters looked at her darkly, and hated her all the more.

6

For many years, the family struggled to survive in their mountain cottage. The three sisters worked every day looking after the sheep and cows. There wasn't a day when her two older sisters didn't groan and moan. Belle never complained, but it was a hard life.

"Things will get better one day, Belle," Marco kept telling her. But he didn't really believe it, and nor did she.

Then, one day, word came that the pirates who'd stolen all Marco's silks, tapestries and spices had been captured. The whole family was overjoyed. As Marco set off to bring back his lost possessions, he told his daughters, "By the time I come home, we'll be rich again. I can bring you whatever you like."

"Diamonds, emeralds and sapphires, lots of them," said the two older sisters.

"And you, Belle?" Marco asked. "What would you like me to bring for you?"

"A red red rose," Belle replied. "No roses grow up here. I love roses."

"All will be well again, my daughters," said Marco, and he rode away down to the coast.

7

But all wasn't well. When Marco arrived at the port, he
discovered that all the silks, tapestries and spices had been
spoilt by sea water. Everything was ruined and worthless.
In deep despair, he made his way back to the mountains
and, on his way, found himself lost in a great dark forest.
Hungry, thirsty and cold, he lay down on the hard,
wet ground and eventually fell asleep.

When he woke, he looked up and saw the towers of a huge
palace through the trees. As he came closer, he saw the front
door was wide open, as if the palace was inviting him in.

Inside, Marco found a huge log fire burning, and a dining table laden with food and drink. There were roasted meats and salted fish, juicy plums and plump pears, mountainous cakes and mouth-watering jellies. Marco sat at the table and ate until he was full to bursting. Then he lay down in front of the fire and was soon fast asleep.

He woke to discover that the table had been laid for breakfast, and helped himself to the food again. Feeling much stronger now, he set off for home.

As he left the palace, Marco found himself in a beautiful rose garden, with red red roses growing all around. He picked three roses, so at least he'd return with something for each of his daughters.

The moment he picked the last rose, there appeared on the path a hideous beast. Huge and horrible he was, with cruel claws and foul breath, and narrow eyes that glared down at him.

"First you steal my food," snarled the beast who had the voice of a wolf. "And now you steal my roses. For this you'll die!"

Marco fell to his knees and begged for mercy. "The food I took because I was starving," he cried. "And the roses I picked for my daughters. They've no one to care for them but me. Spare me for their sake, I beg you."

"Very well," the beast went on, after some thought. "I'll spare you, but only if you send me one of your daughters. You mustn't force her; she must come of her own free will. If none of them will come, then you must return to face whatever fate I've in store for you. Do you promise?"

Marco promised. He'd no choice if he wanted to live. But all the way home he regretted his decision.

Belle was delighted to see her father and loved her red red rose, but her sisters hated theirs. They threw them on the ground and stamped on them, screaming at Marco for returning home as poor as he'd left.

Belle found him later sitting on the mountainside, his head in his hands.

"They don't mean what they say, Father," she said, trying to comfort him.

"They do," Marco replied. "But it's not your sisters' words that are troubling me." Then he told her everything that had happened to him, and everything he'd promised the beast.

"I'll go, Father," she said at once. "I'll be kind to him, and he'll be kind to me because you kept your promise. Everyone is kind deep down. He won't hurt me. Why should he?"

Try as he might to persuade her not to go, Belle insisted. Her sisters, of course, were only too pleased to be rid of her.

As it turned out, Belle was right. When she reached the palace that same evening, the beast couldn't have been more welcoming and kind. She didn't seem to mind one bit what he looked like, and the beast loved her at once for that.

"My palace is your palace," he told her. "And I'll be your willing servant. All I ask in return is that each night you allow me to ask you one question."

Every night, after long and happy days of talking and walking in the rose garden, the beast would ask her the same question: "Dearest Belle, will you marry me?"

And every night she gave him the same answer: "Maybe, but can I think about it just a little longer?"

She did think about it too. She even
dreamt about it, and in her dreams there
was always a handsome prince who lived in
a great palace. This prince kept asking her
that very same question too, and she kept
saying "maybe". These dreams seemed
so real that when Belle woke up she was
sure the prince must be somewhere in
the palace. She started to imagine that
the beast might be keeping the prince
locked up in one of the towers. Of course,
Belle hoped and believed he could never do
such a thing, but she searched every room
in the palace for the prince of her dreams,
just to be sure. But, he wasn't there.

In time, the beast became such a dear and trusted friend to her, that she told him all about her dreams. She even confessed to him how she'd searched the palace. The beast shook his head sadly. "There's no handsome prince here, only me," he told her, looking away so she couldn't see the tears in his eyes.

That night, when the beast asked her yet again to marry him, Belle had a different answer for him. "Dear friend, you've been so kind and patient. I promise that in one week I'll let you know. But before I make up my mind, I'd like to ask my father. Would you mind if I went home for a few days to see him and my sisters? I love being here with you, but I do miss them."

The beast didn't want her to go, but he loved her too much to
keep her against her will. "Go then," he told her, "but keep
your promise and be back in a week with your answer or you'll
break my heart." He gave Belle an enchanted mirror and
a magic ring. "Look into this mirror and you'll be able to see
me and talk to me whenever you like. As for this ring, you only
have to turn it three times around your finger and you'll be
back here with me."

The next morning, Belle left for the mountains. The beast watched her go with a heavy heart. Back at home, Belle told her father all about her wonderful life in the beast's palace: how the beast wanted to marry her, and how she'd promised she'd be back within a week to give him her answer. Marco told her she should go where her heart led her, back to the palace to be with the beast who loved her so much.

Her sisters overheard all
this and were seething
with jealousy. Why should
Belle have all the comforts
of life while they had to stay
home looking after the sheep
and pigs? They'd see to it
that their little sister never
returned to her palace to
become a princess. So they
stole her mirror and her ring
and hid them high in a crow's
nest in the old oak tree by
the stream. Belle looked
everywhere for them, but
couldn't find them.

Then, the sisters thought up a cunning way of making Belle break her promise to the beast. Every morning, as Belle was about to leave, they rubbed onion skins in their eyes to make themselves cry. "Don't go, sister dear," they wept, the tears rolling down their cheeks. "Stay, please stay!" A week and a day went by, then another day and another, and still Belle couldn't bring herself to leave her weeping sisters.

Every night, Belle dreamt again about her handsome prince, only now she was telling him, "Yes, I'll marry you!" But then, one night, she had a different dream altogether. She saw her sisters climbing the old oak tree by the stream. They were hiding away her mirror and her ring high up in a crow's nest.

She woke, ran down to the stream, climbed the tree, and found the mirror and the ring in the nest. There and then she looked into the mirror, and she saw her beloved beast lying in the rose garden of the palace, a red red rose in his hand. With three twists of the ring on her finger, she was kneeling at his side, crying her heart out. As her tears fell on his face, the beast was suddenly a beast no more, but the handsome prince of her dreams. And when his eyes opened and he smiled up at her, Belle thought her heart would burst.

They sat in the rose garden together, and Belle explained how her horrible sisters had tricked her into not keeping her promise. The prince explained how he'd been stolen away by an evil fairy when he was a little boy because she wanted a child of her own. When he'd tried to run away from her, she'd turned him into a hideous beast who could only be made human again if he was ever touched by tears of true love. And now he had been!

Belle and her handsome prince married soon after, and what a wedding it was! Everyone came from miles around. They sang and danced and feasted till the stars faded and the moon became the sun. Her father was there, of course, and her sisters too – Belle had long since forgiven them for the wrong they'd done her. The whole family came to live in the palace and, as it turned out, the sisters proved to be wonderful aunties to Belle's seven children.

But just to remind them of how horrible they'd once been, if ever they needed onions to be cut up for soups and stews, Belle always made her sisters do it. And they wept buckets every time!

Dear Diary,

Well, everything's been so exciting, I don't know where to start! I guess things started to change for the better when Dad lost everything, and we moved to our mountain cottage.

I was so happy there, I didn't want to move ... ever, but when Dad promised a huge, horrible, hideous beast that one of us would go and live with him, I offered. I just couldn't stand to see Dad so sad and worried. And anyway, how bad could it be?

It turns out it wasn't bad at all, but wonderful! The beast wasn't a beast at all, but a lovely, kind and gentle creature and we had such fun together. His palace was amazing and the rose garden – to die for! Apart from the strange dreams I was having, it all seemed pretty perfect.

But, the beast was desperate to get married, and it was such a big decision, I just couldn't do it without my dad's help. So, I went home for a visit. After speaking to Dad, I'd made up my mind to go back, but then I noticed how sad my sisters were, and felt really, really bad.

But, sneaky as they are, it turns out they weren't sad at all. So, I got back to the palace just in time to save my true love's broken heart. And, the biggest shock of all – he isn't a beast at all, but rather a lovely prince! So we got married, and Dad and my sneaky sisters have moved in with us. After all, we've got plenty of space! I can't believe how lucky I am; it just goes to show that all you need in life is love and kindness, and wealth and happiness will follow!

Yours,

Belle

☙ Ideas for reading ☙

Written by Clare Dowdall, PhD
Lecturer and Primary Literacy Consultant

Reading objectives:
- increase familiarity with a wide range of books including fairy stories and retell orally
- identify themes and conventions in a wide range of books
- draw inferences and justify these with evidence

Spoken language objectives:
- give well-structured descriptions, explanations and narratives for different purposes

Curriculum links: PSHE – health and wellbeing; Art – collage with a range of materials

Resources: images from magazines; paper and pens

Build a context for reading
- Ask children to share anything they know about this famous fairy story.
- Look at the characters on the front cover. Ask children to describe what's happening and how the characters might be feeling.
- Read the blurb aloud. Dwell on any unfamiliar language, e.g. "encounters", "doomed", "befriends" and check that children understand the words

Understand and apply reading strategies
- Read pp2–5 to the children. Model reading aloud with expression, and ask children to suggest how the dialogue should be spoken.
- Ask children to recount what they know about Marco, Belle and her sisters, based on the story to that point.
- Ask for a volunteer to read pp6–7 aloud. Discuss how the sisters are different and support children to make inferences by suggesting adjectives that describe Belle and her sisters.
- Ask children to read on to find out if all is well again in Belle and her sisters' lives.